Piranhas

ABDO
Publishing Company

Big Buddy BOOKS
South American Animals

by Julie Murray

VISIT US AT
www.abdopublishing.com

Published by ABDO Publishing Company, PO Box 398166, Minneapolis, Minnesota 55439.

Printed in the United States of America, North Mankato, Minnesota.
092013
012014

 PRINTED ON RECYCLED PAPER

Coordinating Series Editor: Rochelle Baltzer
Editor: Marcia Zappa
Contributing Editors: Megan M. Gunderson, Bridget O'Brien, Sarah Tieck
Graphic Design: Maria Hosley
Cover Photograph: *Photos.com*: Jupiterimages.
Interior Photographs/Illustrations: *Animals Animals-Earth Scenes*: © Ardea/Watson, M. (p. 15); *Getty Images*: Tony Allen (p. 21), ADEK BERRY/AFP (p. 19), Mark Bowler (p. 11), GIUGLIO Gil (p. 5), Werner & Kerstin Layer (p. 29), TOM MCHUGH (p. 23), Andre Seale (p. 15), Paul Zahl/National Geographic (p. 27), Gunter Ziesler (p. 23); *Glow Images*: Steve Bidler/Aflo (p. 8), © John Madere/CORBIS (p. 17); *iStockphoto*: ©iStockphoto.com/ josemoraes (p. 9), ©iStockphoto.com/JohanSjolander (p. 4), ©iStockphoto.com/zxvisual (p. 9); *Minden Pictures*: © Oliver Lucanus/Foto Natura (p. 12), ©Peter Scoones/NPL (p. 25); *Science Source*: Mark Bowler (p. 7), Tom McHugh (p. 9); *Shutterstock*: Ammit Jack (p. 4).

Library of Congress Cataloging-in-Publication Data

Murray, Julie, 1969-
  Piranhas / Julie Murray.
    pages cm. -- (South American animals)
  ISBN 978-1-62403-191-5
1. Piranhas--Juvenile literature. I. Title.
  QL638.C5.M87 2014
  597'.48--dc23
                        2013028913

Contents

Long ago, nearly all land on Earth was one big mass. About 200 million years ago, the land began to break into **continents**. One of these is South America.

Piranhas are famous for their sharp teeth. These fish are also called caribes or pirayas.

South America includes several countries and **cultures**. It is known for its rain forests and interesting animals. One of these animals is the piranha.

Piranha Territory

There are many different types of piranhas. They live throughout **tropical** South America.

Piranhas live in freshwater. They are usually found in fast-moving rivers. But, they also live in lakes and streams. Sometimes, they are found in flooded forests.

Piranha Territory

Scientists are unsure exactly how many types of piranhas there are. Some believe there are more than 60!

Welcome to South America!

If you took a trip to where piranhas live, you might find…

SOUTH

…the Amazon.

The Amazon River is one of the world's largest rivers. It is about 4,000 miles (6,400 km) long! And, the Amazon carries more water than any other river in the world. About 20 different types of piranhas live in this river.

Strait of Magellan

Cape Horn

...tons of fish.

Piranhas aren't the only fish in South America. The Amazon River alone is home to more than 2,000 different types. These include catfish, electric eels, and pirarucu (*right*). Pirarucu can weigh up to 440 pounds (200 kg)!

...a dozen countries.

Twelve countries make up South America. Piranhas live in almost every one! They are especially common in Brazil. This is the largest country in South America in area and population.

Take a Closer Look

Piranhas have tall, thin bodies. An adult may be 5 to more than 24 inches (13 to more than 61 cm) long. They usually weigh less than 8 pounds (4 kg).

A piranha has several stiff **fins**. Its tail is large and strong. This makes it a fast swimmer.

A piranha's belly has a sawlike edge.
This helps it cut through the water.

A piranha's body is covered in scales. Piranhas may be yellowish, olive green, bluish, silver, brown, or black. Many have an orange or red belly.

A piranha's scales help
it hide in the water.

Sharp Teeth

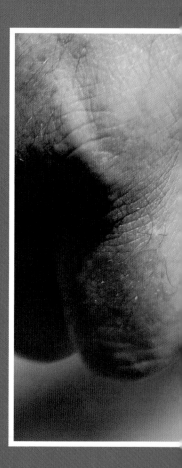

Piranhas are known for their powerful bite. They have strong **jaws**. The upper and lower jaws each have a single line of teeth. These teeth are triangle-shaped and very sharp!

A piranha's teeth are placed close together. When the fish closes its mouth, its teeth lock together. So, its bite makes a clean cut.

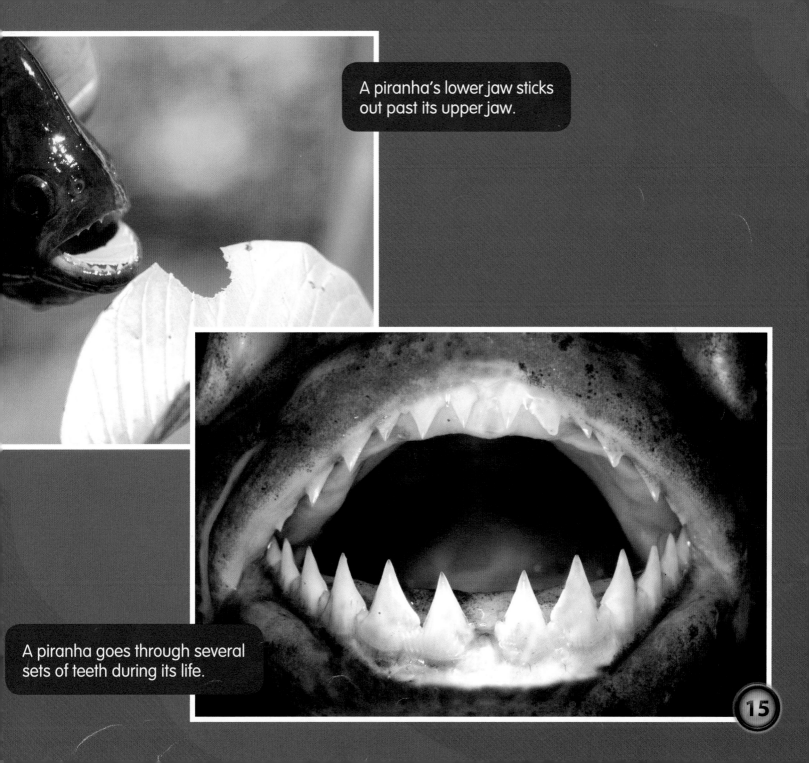

A piranha's lower jaw sticks out past its upper jaw.

A piranha goes through several sets of teeth during its life.

15

Mealtime

Piranhas are famous for having fierce hunting and eating habits. But, this isn't usually the case. Piranhas generally hunt and eat alone. They are most active during the day.

Piranhas eat many different foods. These include smaller fish, worms, snails, insects, water plants, seeds, and fruit. And, they eat **prey** that is already dead.

Uncovered!

A piranha's sharp teeth and powerful jaws allow it to eat prey that is bigger than it is. Most freshwater fish can only eat prey small enough to swallow whole.

Piranhas often eat other fish. Sometimes, this includes other piranhas!

Feeding Frenzy

Sometimes, a group of piranhas come together to attack and eat large **prey**. This is known as a feeding frenzy. Feeding frenzies generally take place during the dry season. At this time, the bodies of water piranhas live in are smaller than usual. Piranhas become packed close together. And, food is hard to find.

Uncovered!
Feeding frenzies sometimes occur when piranhas smell blood in the water.

A feeding frenzy may include more than 100 piranhas!

When food is hard to find, piranhas will attack almost anything they can. This includes large **prey**, such as **capybaras**. Piranhas take turns using their sharp teeth to take bites out of their prey. They do this very quickly. In a feeding frenzy, even large prey can be eaten in just minutes!

Uncovered!
Only a few types of piranhas attack large prey. They very rarely attack humans.

During a feeding frenzy, the water may bubble and splash. Some say it looks like the water is boiling.

21

Safety in Numbers

Piranhas often swim in groups called schools or shoals. Swimming in groups helps keep them safe from predators. These include otters, caimans, water snakes, turtles, birds, larger fish, and river dolphins. Humans also hunt piranhas.

Young piranhas are especially likely to be attacked. But, even fully-grown adults have predators.

Piranhas stay close together when they swim in schools.

23

Incredible Eggs

During the rainy season, a pair of piranhas moves to slow-moving water to **mate**. The pair, or just the male, makes a shallow, round nest on the ground. Then, the female lays about 5,000 eggs in the nest.

Uncovered!
About 90 percent of piranha eggs hatch. That is more than most fish.

A piranha pair guards its nest closely.

Baby Piranhas

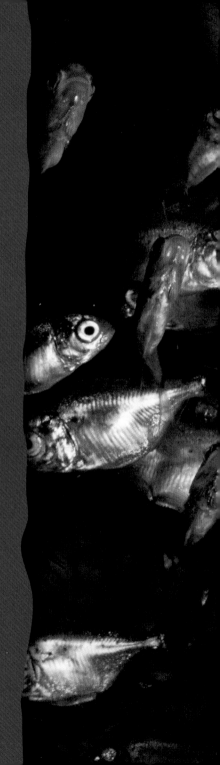

After two to ten days, piranha eggs **hatch**. Newly hatched piranhas look similar to adults. But, they are much smaller and often have differently colored scales.

At first, they stay hidden among water plants. They eat small bugs, worms, fruit, and seeds. After they are about one and a half inches (4 cm) long, they begin to journey farther. And, they start to hunt larger **prey**.

At zoos, young piranhas eat different foods than they would in the wild. Sometimes, they are fed ground meat.

Survivors

Life in South America isn't easy for piranhas. People and animals hunt them for food. **Prey** can be hard to find. And, people often capture piranhas to sell as pets.

Still, piranhas **survive**. In fact, many types can be found in large numbers! Piranhas help make South America an amazing place.

In the wild, piranhas can live for up to 12 years.

Wow!
I'll bet you never knew...

...that piranha teeth are useful in different ways. Native people use them to make tools and weapons.

...that piranhas have been found in the wild outside of South America. When pet owners decide they no longer want their piranhas, they sometimes let them go in the wild. This can be dangerous for local fish, frogs, and other animals.

...that piranhas are named for their sharp teeth. Their name comes from native words for "fish," *pira*, and "tooth," *sanha*.

Important Words

capybara (ka-pih-BEHR-uh) a large, tailless South American rodent that is often found in or near water.

continent one of Earth's seven main land areas.

culture (KUHL-chuhr) the arts, beliefs, and ways of life of a group of people.

fin a body part of a water animal shaped like a blade or fan. Fins are used to move or guide the animal through water.

hatch to be born from an egg.

jaws a mouthpart that allows for holding, crushing, and chewing.

mate to join as a couple in order to reproduce, or have babies.

prey an animal hunted or killed by a predator for food.

survive to continue to live or exist.

tropical of or relating to parts of the world where temperatures are warm and the air is moist all the time.

Web Sites

To learn more about piranhas, visit ABDO Publishing Company online. Web sites about piranhas are featured on our Book Links page. These links are routinely monitored and updated to provide the most current information available.

www.abdopublishing.com

Index